Joe Biden $1.9 Trillion Economic Rescue Plan

THE JOE BIDEN POLICIES, STRATEGIES, TARGET TO COMBACT COVID 19/OTHER CRISIS AND RESCUE AMERICAN ECONOMIC FROM RECESSION

Dr. Joe Bama

Copyright© 2021 Dr. Joe Bama

All Right Reserved

TABLE OF CONTENTS

INTROUCTION

WHAT'S IN THE PROPOSITION?

THE ECONOMY NEEDS ASSISTANCE.

MR. BIDEN IS PULLING OUT ALL THE STOPS.

HERE'S WHAT'S HAPPENING

A GUARD BENEFIT FOR AMERICA'S GREATEST BANK.

TRY NOT TO EXPECT LOAN FEE CLIMBS ANY TIME SOON, JAY POWELL SAYS.

Palantir's Covid-19 global positioning framework experiences harsh criticism.

Jim Simons ventures down as director of Renaissance Technology.

BlackRock gets much greater.

Another 'diagram' for Fannie and Freddie

IBM proposes 'post-rebellion changes'

Depository curves to a crypto fight arrangements

GOVERNMENTAL ISSUES AND STRATEGY

TECH

MOST AWESOME ASPECT THE REST

INTROUCTION

President-elect Joe Biden revealed his $1.9 trillion monetary salvage plan, an eager bundle of greater direct installments to Americans, additional subsidizing for Covid immunization conveyance and that's just the beginning. The move is a bolder reaction than the Obama organization's to the 2008 monetary emergency — regardless of whether it adds to the obligation to bewildering levels.

What's in the proposition?

- **$1,400 direct installments,** a $15 every hour government the lowest pay permitted by law and more liberal joblessness benefits.

- <u>**$400 billion to battle the pandemic straightforwardly,**</u> including quickening antibody sending and returning most schools inside 100 days of entry. (Today, Mr. Biden declared that Dr. David Kessler, a previous F.D.A. boss who has co-led his

Covid team, would assume control over the Operation Warp Speed antibody appropriation activity.)

- **$350 billion for state and nearby governments** to connect spending setbacks.

The economy needs assistance. The Labor Department announced that 1.15 million Americans documented new joblessness claims in the principal entire seven day stretch of the new year, the most significant level since July.

Mr. Biden is pulling out all the stops. The spending would come on top of the $2 trillion alleviation bill from March and the $900 billion help program in December. Paradoxically, the focal point of the Obama organization's reaction to the monetary emergency checked in at around $800 billion.

The bundle would be financed totally with acquiring. Numerous financial analysts have asked policymakers to put aside worries about deficiencies, and Mr. Biden has all the earmarks of being paying attention to those contentions. He recognized that his arrangement "doesn't come efficiently," however contended that doing less "will cost us truly." Interest rates and swelling aren't squeezing concerns, a few financial specialists contend, so more forceful measures to support the recuperation could all the more rapidly open the repressed interest and investment funds developed during pandemic lockdowns.

- This time around, Mr. Biden has prevailed upon bunches like the U.S. Office of Commerce, which regularly restricted Obama-time financial activities. "We hail the duly elected president's

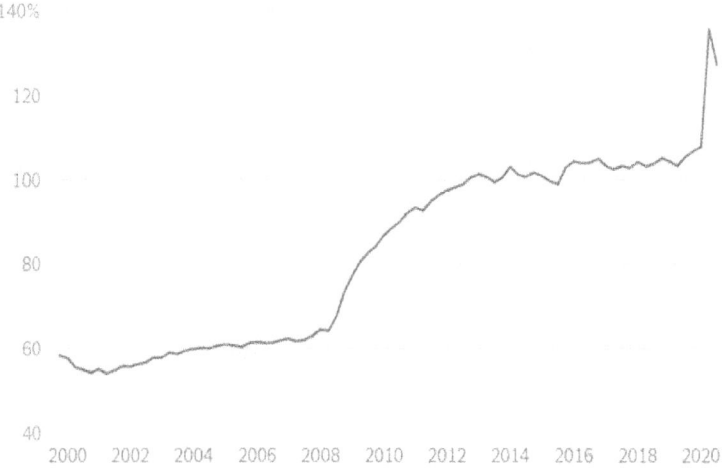

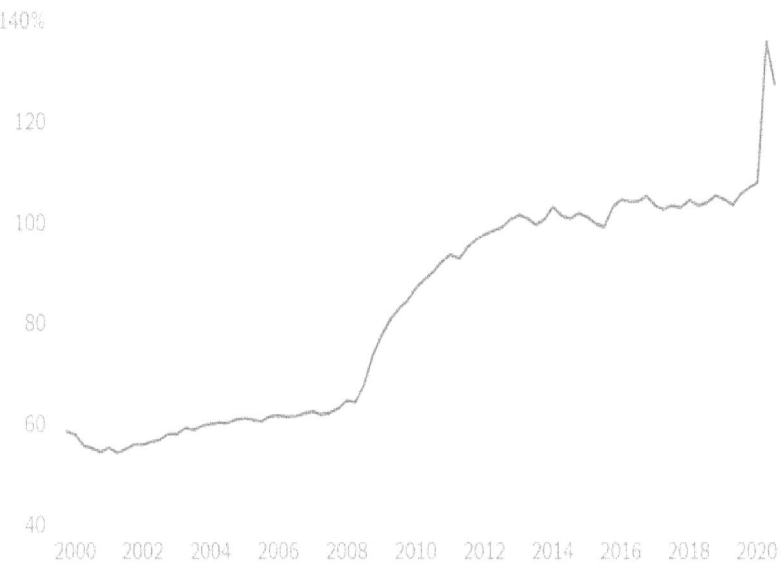

Ratio of U.S. public debt to G.D.P.

Source: U.S. Office of Management and Budget • By The New York Times

In any case, entry through Congress isn't guaranteed. With Democrats set to manage the House and the Senate, Mr. Biden is wagering that he can beat Republicans' earlier refusals to think about greater financial plans. Yet, Democrats' control of the Senate is thin, and Mr. Biden would need to counterbalance any possible deserters with help from Republican conservatives.

HERE'S WHAT'S HAPPENING

<u>A guard benefit for America's greatest bank.</u> JPMorgan Chase commenced Wall Street's income season today with a record $12.1 billion benefit in its most recent quarter, up in excess of 40% from the prior year. Essentially the entirety of the association's business lines beat assumptions, particularly its venture banking and exchanging activities.

Try not to expect loan fee climbs any time soon, Jay Powell says. The Fed seat said that the national bank is set up to raise rates "when the opportunity arrives," yet is probably not going to do as such while the economy is as yet delicate, regardless of whether swelling rises this year.

Palantir's Covid-19 global positioning framework experiences harsh criticism. C.D.C. authorities told individuals from President-elect Joe Biden's progress group that the information mining association's drive, which is intended to follow clinics' reactions to the pandemic continuously, is incorrect, The Daily Beast reports.

Jim Simons ventures down as director of Renaissance Technology. The mutual funds financial specialist, who established Renaissance in 1982, is giving the title to the association's C.E.O., Peter Brown. The pioneer in PC driven putting endured twofold digit misfortunes in assets open to outside speculators a year ago.

BlackRock gets much greater. The speculation the board goliath currently supervises almost $8.7 trillion, it said while declaring a 19 percent hop in quarterly profit. The outcomes underline the force of the company's establishment as it utilizes its size to box out more modest opponents.

Another 'diagram' for Fannie and Freddie

Fannie Mae and Freddie Mac, the public authority supported home loan account firms, won't be privatized when the Biden organization dominates, as the Trump organization's Federal Housing Finance Agency chief, Mark Calabria, had planned. All things considered, the Treasury Department reported that it will permit the endeavors — which are managed by the F.H.F.A. — to hold more benefits and assemble their capital stores. This gives "an outline that we expect will help manage extra changes," the

Treasury stated, alluding to a way to privatization.

Mr. Calabria is resolved to privatization, yet it requires the understanding of the Treasury, which possesses favored portions of Fannie and Freddie in the wake of rescuing them in the 2008 subprime loaning emergency. Hurrying to deliver the gatherings from government control would have been unsafe and problematic, said Mr. Parrot, a previous senior counsel on lodging issues in the Obama organization.

The progressions are "unassuming" and nonbinding, fundamentally bookkeeping changes, said Mark Zandi, the central financial specialist of Moody's Analytics. Furthermore, they won't direct what the following Treasury secretary can do, which is something worth being thankful for in Mr. Zandi's view. Semi administrative status has permitted Fannie and Freddie to be more adaptable about broadening acknowledge, just as abandonment and removal bans, during the pandemic than if they were simply private.

IBM proposes 'post-rebellion changes'

IBM declared a progression of suggestions for government strategy changes in the wake of the Jan. 6 viciousness at the Capitol. They incorporate more clear direction around official changes, stricter guidelines on monetary revelations for officeholders and the sky is the limit from there. The tech monster's support is imperative in light of the fact that these issues aren't connected straightforwardly to its business and they're not sponsored by any corporate political gifts, which IBM has illegal for over a century.

"Companies' thought process is strategy changes, not PAC checks," Christopher Padilla, IBM's VP of government and administrative issues, composed on the organization's blog."Rather than just suspending PAC responsibilities as a sign sending exercise, what looks good for us, since we don't do political responsibilities, is to endeavor to change government such that will keep a portion of this stuff from occurring later on," he told DealBook.

- Despite shunning direct gifts, IBM is a functioning lobbyist and hasn't shied from recruiting individuals with political ties, including most as of late

Gary Cohn, President Trump's previous financial counselor, as bad habit administrator.

Workers and investors anticipate that organizations should be "dependable players," Mr. Padilla stated, "and that is the thing that we're attempting to do." IBM representatives had squeezed the organization to stand up after the brutality in the Capitol, much as they did after George Floyd's murder a year ago. Following Mr. Floyd's passing, the organization called for changes to police strategy and said it would escape the facial acknowledgment business.

Depository curves to a crypto fight

After an objection from digital currency allies and their partners in Congress, the Treasury Department today will resume the remark time frame for proposed advanced cash detailing decides that it says are planned to forestall tax evasion. Its unique remark period was 15 days, over the special seasons, an abnormally short window that the Blockchain Association, a crypto exchange gathering, would presumably have tested in court. "This doesn't resolve the make a difference, yet it stops the mischief this standard would have caused had it become effective," the affiliation said.

Presently, the crypto sponsor has more opportunity to say something, and a renewed individual to campaign. They won an additional 15 days to remark on principles for certain "unhosted" advanced wallet exchanges, and 45 additional days for proposed necessities on "facilitated" wallet clients. Along these lines, Steven Mnuchin will presently don't be showing the Treasury Department to the time it thinks about the remarks, which may satisfy the crypto swarm.

At the point when she led the Fed, Janet Yellen said existing illegal tax avoidance rules were "satisfactory to address authorization issues," in a discourse about advanced monetary standards in 2014. Presently, she is the Biden organization's candidate for Treasury secretary. In view of her record, she might be open to reconsidering the proposed rule changes. The Blockchain Association's leader chief, Kristin Smith, disclosed to Fortune that Joe Biden's success in November was "something to be thankful for" for digital money.

Arrangements

- Investors like BlackRock and Silver Lake are left with billion-dollar stakes in Ant Group that they can't sell after Chinese controllers subdued the tech monster's I.P.O. plans. (FT)

- Goldman Sachs is allegedly thinking about significant acquisitions to reinforce Marcus, the association's shopper banking arm. (Reuters)

- The dissident speculation firm Kimmeridge has gotten one of the main 10 speculators in the energy organization Ovinitiv and plans to start an intermediary battle about its ecological record. (Kimmeridge)

Governmental issues and strategy

- The pandemic is required to cost New York City $2.5 billion in lost local charge income one year from now. (NYT)

- Shares in the cell phone producer Xiaomi plunged after the Trump organization moved to banish Americans from putting resources into it over supposed connections to the Chinese military. (CNBC)

- Trump White House staff individuals are getting the brush off when searching for occupations in corporate America. (Business Insider)

Tech

- TikTok will outlive the Trump organization. Be that as it may, how the Biden organization will treat it — and Chinese tech organizations all the more extensively — is hazy. (NYT)

- After suspending President Trump's records, Facebook and Twitter are feeling the squeeze from basic liberties backers to do likewise to other well-known individuals blamed for inciting brutality. (NYT)

- Microsoft, Oracle, and Salesforce have joined a gathering that is creating tech principles for advanced inoculation identifications. (NYT)

Most awesome aspect the rest

- "Is Remote Work Making Us Paranoid?" (NYT)

- Macaulay Culkin, the star of "Home Alone 2," joined calls to have President Trump's appearance altered out of the 1992 film. (The Hill)

The story that has been getting all over town in Washington: "The $3,000-a-month lavatory for the Ivanka Trump/Jared Kushner Secret Service detail" (WaPo)

www.ingramcontent.com/pod-product-compliance
Lightning Source LLC
Chambersburg PA
CBHW050323220526
45465CB00005B/2104